Practise it

Complete and then copy the sentences using your usual joi[ned]

Let me introduce myself. My name is _____.

I would describe my handwriting as _____.

I have my own unique signature: _____.

Apply it

Use the phrases below to write a short account of an entertaining event. It could be real or imaginary. Use your usual joined handwriting.

You will never believe what happened to me last Saturday.

First of all, ...   *Before long, ...*
After that, ...   *Eventually, ...*

Book 11 | Style

Looping for style

You may find that looping to or from certain letters with tails makes your handwriting smoother and more fluent. Make sure your loops are consistent and not too big.

If you find looping awkward, do not loop. Lifting your pen after the letters **g**, **y** and **j** may help your fluency. Decide which option works best for you.

looping: *jumping jellyfish*　　not looping: *jumping jellyfish*

Try it

1. Copy and continue the letter patterns using looping joins.

    gygy

    ylyl

    juji

    cycy

    ggng

2. Copy each word twice with and twice without looping joins. Find your preferred style of joining.

    energy

    foreign

    judged

    cylinder

    signed

    polygon

    pyjamas

Practise it

Copy the headings using your preferred style of joining.

Enjoy growing vegetables

Try Olympic-style cycling

Beginner's guide to yoga

Studying foreign languages

Teach yourself geography

Apply it

Write a noun to complete the subject of each alliterative sentence. Then copy the sentences using your preferred style of joining and write one of your own.

A _____ *gorged greedily on grey gooey grubs.*

A _____ *judged the gymnast's jumps as jolly jerky.*

A _____ *yanked the yawning yeti off a yellow yacht.*

A _____ *jingled jewels and gems in a giant jam jar.*

A _____ *greets gory ghouls in a gloomy graveyard.*

A _____ *yearns for yummy yams and yoghurts.*

Book 11 | Style

Joining break letters b, p, s

You can choose to join **b**, **p** and **s** to the next letter by retracing along the lower curve. This may improve the fluency and flow of your handwriting.

However, if these joins feel awkward or result in badly shaped letters, leave them unjoined. For you, pen lifts after **b**, **p** and **s** may feel more fluent.

joined break letters: *purple bruises*   unjoined break letters: *purple bruises*

Try it

1. Copy and continue the letter patterns using joins from the letters **b**, **p** and **s**.

    bbt

    ppy

    sso

    spt

    phb

2. Copy each word twice with and twice without joins from the letters **b**, **p** and **s**. Find your preferred style of joining.

    bruise

    doubt

    erupts

    harass

    social

    phrase

    poppy

Practise it

Copy the tongue-twisters using your preferred style of joining.

a bit of butter for the batter

Plump pickled peppers pop.

"Hisssss," said a sea snake.

Poppy's puppies are popular.

Apply it

Copy the sentences, choosing the correct homophone. Use your preferred style of joining. Then complete the final sentence.

Do people eat grapes for breakfast or **dessert/desert**?

Inside the pyramid was a system of **symbols/cymbals**.

Did people have solar power in the **past/passed**?

I am happy to **accept/except** my brother's apology.

We must see a script to **practise/practice** the play.

The seaside **peer/pier** is a popular place to be.

Did the robber **steel/steal** …

Book 11 I Style

Joining break letters q, x, z

It can be useful to have some break letters in your writing, particularly when joining longer words. The pen lift allows you to move your hand and arm along.

However, you may choose to join all your letters, even **q**, **x** and **z**, moving your hand as you write. Make sure your letter shapes remain clear and that size and spacing are consistent.

joined break letters: *technique*   unjoined break letters: *technique*

Try it

1 Copy and continue the letter patterns with joins for the letters **q**, **x** and **z**.

qu _____   equ _____

ex _____   ux _____

za _____   zo _____

2 Copy each word twice with and twice without joins for the letters **q**, **x** and **z**. Remember, only join <u>to</u> the letter **x** and <u>from</u> the letter **z**. Find your preferred style of joining.

technique _____   _____

exterior _____   _____

horizon _____   _____

equality _____   _____

frequent _____   _____

luxury _____   _____

complex _____   _____

hazard _____   _____

Practise it

Copy the sentences using your preferred style of joining.

The chimpanzee frequently exercised on the trapeze.

A trapezium is a quadrilateral with two parallel sides.

Apply it

Copy the police report, choosing the more formal word to complete each sentence. Use your preferred style of joining.

After **examining**/looking at all the available evidence, it appears the suspect entered the property at about/**approximately** 11 p.m. and then/**subsequently** broke into the victim's safe. The suspect has offered no satisfactory explanation for how she **acquired**/got the golden nuggets. **Consequently,**/So, we have no alternative but to inform the relevant authorities and ask for/**request** a speedy trial.

Book 11 | Style

Rounded v and w

Letter shapes can be wide and rounded or narrow and oval, but they should always be consistent.

Some people choose to write the letters **v** and **w** with a more rounded shape. If you prefer this style, make sure your letters are legible. Check that your rounded **v** does not look like a **u**.

rounded: ʋ w   not rounded: v w

Try it

1. Copy and continue the letter patterns using a rounded **v** and **w**.

   ʋʋʋʋʋ

   wwwww

   vovovo

   wowowo

   vavava

   wawawa

2. Copy each word twice with and twice without a rounded **v** and **w**. Find your preferred style of letter shape.

   savage

   wonder

   voyage

   swarm

   canvas

Practise it

Copy the sentences using your preferred style of letter shape.

Several swallows warbled in the waterlogged wood.

The woman vowed to visit a volcano on her voyage.

Apply it

Copy the story, choosing the correct spelling to complete each sentence. Use your preferred style of letter shape. Then add a sentence of your own.

Alvin the **awkward/aukward** aardvark wanted an awesome adventure. He wanted to **wonder/wander** the savannah and discover the wide, wide world. He was **weary/weiry** of living in dark tunnels and would welcome the warmth of the sun.

You see, Alvin was not your **average/avarage** aardvark. He didn't even like termites! Alvin wanted some **varierty/variety**.

Book 11 | Style

Slanting for style

You may choose to slant your writing slightly to the right to improve your fluency and flow. If you choose a slanted style, make sure the slant is consistent and not too extreme.

If you find slanting difficult or uncomfortable, use an upright style, but be consistent. Remember that all downstrokes should be parallel.

slanted style   slightly slanted

Try it

1. Copy and continue the letter patterns with a slant.

   fulful

   illill

   ultult

   htnhtn

2. Copy each word twice with a slant and twice upright. Find your preferred style of joining. Remember, keep your slant consistent.

   slightly

   ultimate

   difficulty

   illegally

   truthfully

   immortal

   definitely

   lightning

Practise it

Copy the rhyming sentence three times using your preferred style of joining.

Thirty days hath September, April, June and November.

Apply it

Write the adverb **Fortunately** or **Unfortunately** at the start of each sentence. Remember to use a comma after the adverb. Then copy the story using your preferred style of joining and add two sentences of your own to complete it.

Mr Hardluck usually liked to take a walk at lunchtime.
_____, *today it began to rain almost immediately.*
_____ *Mr Hardluck had an umbrella with him.*
_____ *the umbrella was struck by lightning.*
_____ *Mr Hardluck was unhurt, although he was a little shocked by what had happened.*

Book 11 | Style

Printing

Sometimes an unjoined print style of lettering is used instead of joined handwriting. Print letters are used when words need to be particularly clear and easy to read – for example, labels on a diagram or words on a poster.

Print letters do not have flicks. They are upright, not slanted. When printing, straight forms of the letters **f** and **k** are used.

the print letters f and k

Try it

1 Copy the alphabet twice using print letters.

Aa Bb Cc Dd Ee Ff Gg Hh Ii Jj Kk Ll Mm

Nn Oo Pp Qq Rr Ss Tt Uu Vv Ww Xx Yy Zz

2 Copy the names of the countries and continents using clear print letters.

Brazil _____   China _____

Mexico _____   Pakistan _____

Egypt _____   Germany _____

Sweden _____   Denmark _____

Nigeria _____ Canada _____

Africa _____   Europe _____

Practise it

Copy the headings using print letters.

The human skeleton

The digestive system

The function of blood cells

The work of muscles

Apply it

Use the words from the box to label the diagram using print letters.

*spine
(backbone)*

*cranium
(skull)*

*femur
(thigh bone)*

*patella
(kneecap)*

*scapula
(shoulder
blade)*

Book 11 | Style

17

Block capitals

Sometimes words are written using only capital letters, with each letter written separately and clearly. This style of writing is called block capitals.

Block capitals are used when words need to be particularly clear and legible, such as when filling in a form, or to make certain words stand out, such as on a poster or a leaflet.

CAPITAL LETTERS

Try it

1 Write the alphabet twice using block capitals. Keep the letters the same size as you write. The first alphabet should be bigger than the second.

A B _____

_____

A B _____

_____

2 Copy each word using block capitals.

reduced _____   library _____

bargains _____   festival _____

exclusive _____   entrance _____

discount _____   staring _____

surprise _____   amazing _____

missing _____   superb _____

caution _____   incredible _____

wanted _____   beware _____

Practise it

Copy the phrases on to the poster using block capitals. Use four different sizes of lettering, one for each line.

Visit Melbury Hall

Lots of special events

Open April to December

Free entry for children

Apply it

Complete the entry form for a painting competition. Use block capitals to fill in your details.

COMPETITION ENTRY FORM

Full name: _____

Class: _____ Teacher: _____

School: _____

School address: _____

Home address: _____

Title of painting: _____

Book 11 | Style

Choosing writing tools

There are many writing tools: pencils, ballpoint pens, ink or fountain pens, fine liners, felt-tip pens, rollerballs, markers, crayons and gel pens.

Different writing tools have different qualities. This can affect the size, style and quality of your writing. It is important to choose the correct writing tool for a particular task.

thin line, smaller letters: fine liner   wide line, larger letters: **THICK MARKER**

Try it

1. Explore a selection of writing tools. Copy and continue the letter pattern using a different writing tool each time. Think about the qualities of each tool and what kind of writing you would use it for.

   abcdef _____
   abcdef _____
   abcdef _____
   abcdef _____
   abcdef _____
   abcdef _____

2. Copy the words, using an appropriate writing tool for each one.

   fine _____   thick _____
   colourful _____   bold _____
   scratchy _____   smooth _____
   hard _____   soft _____
   fluid _____   clear _____
   heavy _____   narrow _____

Practise it

Copy the writing tasks, using an appropriate writing tool and style for each one.

writing on a flipchart _____

creating decorative borders _____

making rough notes _____

presenting my best writing _____

Apply it

Use the ideas in the box and some of your own to create a poster about staying safe in the sun, aimed at young children. Use at least three different writing tools.

BE SUN-SMART

Wear a sunhat.

Drink water.

Wear sun cream.

Seek shade.

Rays from the sun can be harmful to skin and eyes.

Stay safe this summer.

Decorative lettering

Sometimes a special decorative style of lettering is used for a specific purpose – for example, in a title, on a poster or in a shape poem.

The basic letters are still recognisable, but their shape is adapted or details are added so that the style of lettering represents the subject.

curly   **wabbly**   *speedy*

Try it

1. Copy the letters in the different styles of decorative lettering. Choose writing tools that are suitable for the task.

   Aa Bb Cc Dd Ee Ff Gg Hh

   Ii Jj Kk Ll Mm Nn Oo Pp Qq

   Rr Ss Tt Uu Vv Ww Xx Yy Zz

2. Copy the words in the correct style of decorative lettering. Use colour and different writing tools if you wish.

   curly _____   wabbly _____

   speedy _____   FLUFFY _____

   bouncy _____   stringy _____

   square _____   dotty _____

Practise it

Copy the book titles using a suitable decorative style of lettering to represent each subject.

Tales of Magic

Turbo the Robot

101 Dalmatians

Shiver and Shake

Apply it

Add the missing antonyms to the poem. Then copy it using a suitable decorative style of lettering for each word or phrase on a line. Choose suitable writing tools for the task and use colour if you wish.

Letters can be fat,
Letters can be _____,
Letters can be bubbles,
Or even coloured in.
Letters can be fancy,
Letters can be _____,
Letters can have stripes,
Or even drip with rain.
Letters can be short,
Letters can be _____,
Letters can be bold,
Or hardly there at all.

Book 11 | Style

Calligraphy

Calligraphy is the art of beautiful handwriting. It is used to produce special handwritten texts.

Ink pens or brushes are used to draw letters using thick and thin strokes. The basic shapes are the same as in standard handwriting, but the letters have flourishes (extra curves and flicks) to make them more decorative.

calligraphy

Try it

1 Copy the alphabet using a calligraphy style of lettering. Try a range of writing tools to find one suitable for the task.

Aa Bb Cc Dd Ee Ff Gg Hh Ii

Jj Kk Ll Mm Nn Oo Pp Qq Rr

Ss Tt Uu Vv Ww Xx Yy Zz

2 Copy the words using print letters and then a calligraphy style of lettering.

castle	_____	*castle*	_____
ancient	_____	*ancient*	_____
dragons	_____	*dragons*	_____
scroll	_____	*scroll*	_____
sword	_____	*sword*	_____
kingdom	_____	*kingdom*	_____

Practise it

Copy the phrases using a calligraphy style of lettering.

Visit Warwick Castle

Dragon Kingdom

By royal invitation

Congratulations

Apply it

Complete the certificate for a deserving person. Then copy it using a calligraphy style of lettering. Add patterns or illustrations.

Certificate of achievement

awarded to

_____

for excellence in

_____

Book 11 | Style

Choosing your standard of handwriting

Different situations require different standards of handwriting. When you start a writing task, choose an appropriate speed and standard of presentation. Decide whether speed is more important or the quality of the handwriting.

Often, writing needs to be both fast and easily legible. Some attention must be given to quality, while still maintaining speed.

speed ➔ personal notes

presentation ➔ writing for display

Try it

1. Copy the sentences twice using an appropriate standard of handwriting.

   This is my very fastest writing, which I use for notes.

   This writing is fast but legible to other readers.

2. Copy each task into the correct list to show the standard of handwriting needed.

   writing a report   jotting ideas   writing instructions
   making notes   a phone message   personal reminder

   Fast but easily legible   **Very fast and only read by me**

Practise it

Copy the sentences as if they are answers in a timed test. Use a suitable standard of handwriting.

The bulb will be brighter. _____

'His' is a possessive pronoun. _____

They are all invertebrates. _____

He was a world champion. _____

Apply it

Write the information as a quick note for yourself and then as a bullet-point list for parents. Write quickly, choosing a suitable standard of handwriting for each task. You could use abbreviations in your note.

Make sure you have everything you need on Wednesday. It might rain so bring a coat, ideally one that is waterproof, and a pair of outdoor shoes or boots. We will be out all day so you need a packed lunch, including a drink. A rucksack would be useful. Please bring no more than five pounds to spend.

Note to myself

Wed

List for parents

We need these items on Wednesday:
-

Book 11 | Style

Your best handwriting

Best handwriting takes time and care. It must be clear, consistent and attractive.

Use your best handwriting on occasions when quality is important – for example, a final or best copy made once editing and proofreading are complete. Focus on the handwriting and take your time so that there are no errors.

Best handwriting takes time and care.

Try it

1 Copy the sentences in your very best handwriting.

I am proud to show my best handwriting.

I produce best copies that look attractive.

2 Read the list and choose four occasions when you would use your best handwriting. Copy them carefully on to the diagram.

final copy of a poem

answers in a test

writing for a display

problems in maths

writing competition

letter to the Queen

notes made in science

shopping list

best handwriting

Practise it

Write a final version of the edited text. Use your best handwriting.

He was being sucked towards the rapids, floundering in a whirlpool of foam. His clothes, drenched with icy water, clung to him, dragging him down.

Apply it

Write a synonym to improve each crossed-out word in the character description. Then copy it in your best handwriting.

Ms Blake was ~~funny~~ _____ and had a really infectious laugh. She could be a bit eccentric and sometimes wore ~~odd~~ _____ clothes – but that was just her personality. She was very ~~brainy~~ _____ and her lessons were always fascinating. Her pupils were always very ~~keen~~ _____ – everyone wanted to be in Ms Blake's class.

Book 11 | Style

Proofreading and punctuation

Check punctuation as part of proofreading. Make sure your punctuation marks are placed at the correct height in relation to letters.

Colons and semicolons should be placed around the height of short letters. Dashes and hyphens should be placed between the baseline and short letter line.

Name: Anne-Marie

Try it

1 Copy and continue the patterns. Remember that a hyphen is shorter than a dash.

re-co-re-co-

oo — oo —

I:I:I: I:I:I:

(;) / (;) /

!!!... !!!...

2 Copy the phrases and sentences.

Name: Anne-Marie

I like art; Joe does too.

a pop-up picture book

This is my dog – he's cute.

(speaking to the audience)

Something was wrong …

What a brilliant goal!

Who was the co-pilot?

Practise it

Copy each sentence, adding the colon, hyphen or semicolon in the correct place.

I looked inside the bag a book, pencils and a letter.

Colon: _____

I have a lovely long haired rabbit called Benjamin.

Hyphen: _____

I've never been skiing before I'm very excited.

Semicolon: _____

Apply it

The paragraph is missing a colon, a hyphen and a semicolon. Proofread the paragraph, adding one punctuation mark to each sentence. Then copy the paragraph in your best handwriting.

Think about the water you use in a day there is washing, cleaning, showering, cooking and, of course, drinking. Even in the twenty first century, many countries do not have running water. We have water to waste they have none. How can that be fair?

Book 11 I Style

Presentation and layout

Good presentation and a clear layout can help make your handwriting look more attractive.

Handwriting should be well spaced. Use margins, borders and line spaces. You might choose to centre text rather than starting on the left.

Use patterns, decorative borders or illustrations to add visual impact.

෴ **Spring Poem** ෴
centred text

Try it

1. Copy and continue the decorative patterns using a suitable writing tool.

2. Copy the acrostic poem so it is in the centre of the lines rather than on the left.

Sunlight,

Pollen and

Rainbows.

Incredible

New life and

Greenness.

Practise it

Copy the text on to the invitation, choosing how to position and space the text. Add illustrations or a border around the edge.

You are invited to celebrate Michael's 11th birthday on Saturday 12th August at 3 p.m. at Woodlands Activity Centre. Full directions are enclosed. RSVP

Party

Apply it

Find a short poem to include in an anthology of favourite children's poems. Copy the poem and present it attractively. Choose suitable writing tools.

WriteWell challenge 1

Copy the extract from a poem by Walter de La Mare in your best joined handwriting. Present the poem attractively and set it out clearly. Add patterns or illustrations.

> If I were Lord of Tartary,
> Myself and me alone,
> My bed should be of ivory,
> Of beaten gold my throne;
> And in my court should peacocks flaunt,
> And in my forests tigers haunt,
> And in my pools great fishes slant
> Their fins athwart the sun.

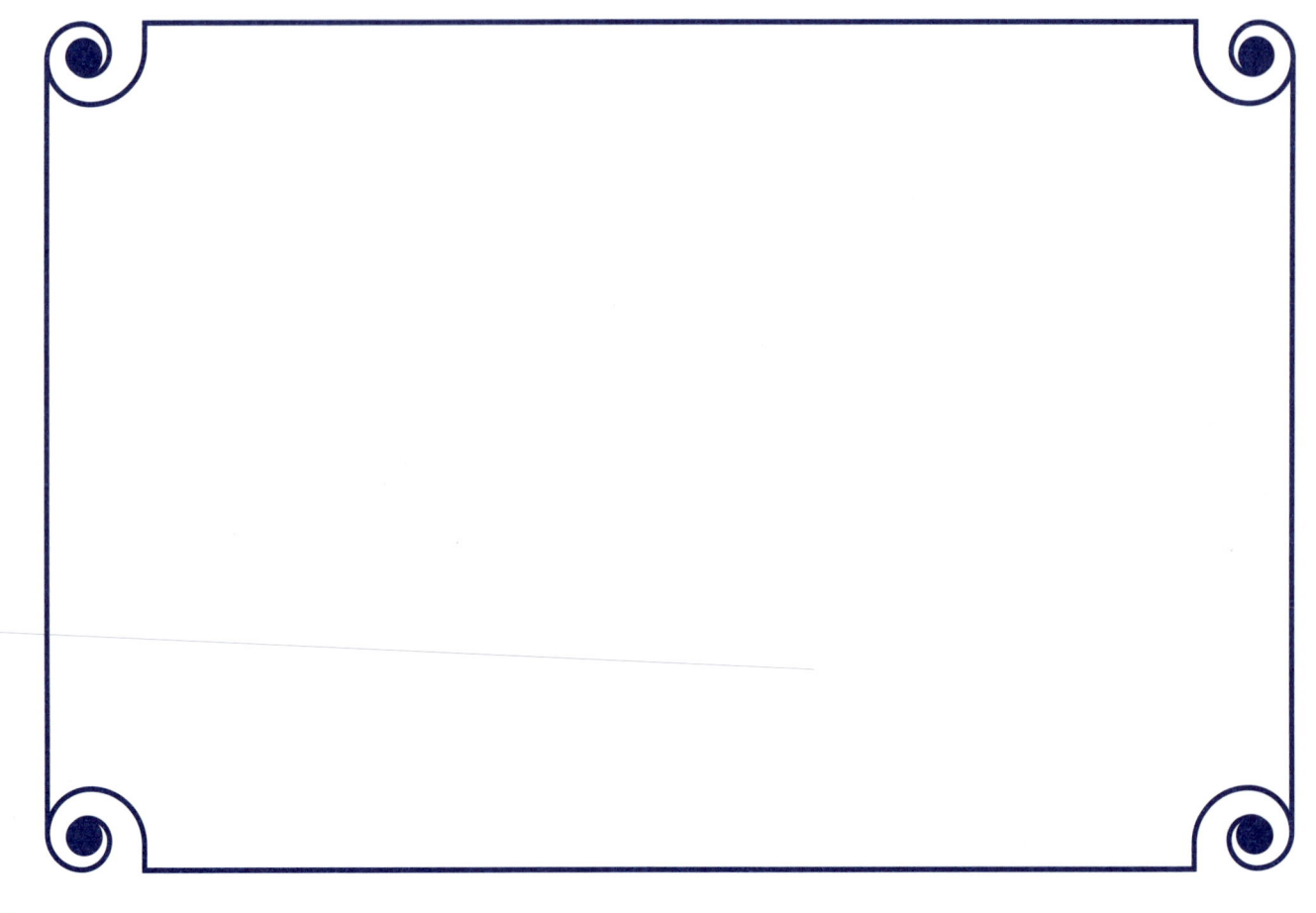